T0066046

CANCER

June 21 – July 22

Image by Andrea Lauren © Simon & Schuster, Inc.

A
good head and
a good heart
are always a
formidable
combination

✧ Nelson Mandela ✧

Image by Andrea Lauren © Simon & Schuster, Inc.

Images by Andrea Lauren © Simon & Schuster, Inc., and 123RF/Volodymyr Horbovyy

IRIS

Image by Andrea Lauren © Simon & Schuster, Inc.

Image by Andrea Lauren © Simon & Schuster, Inc.

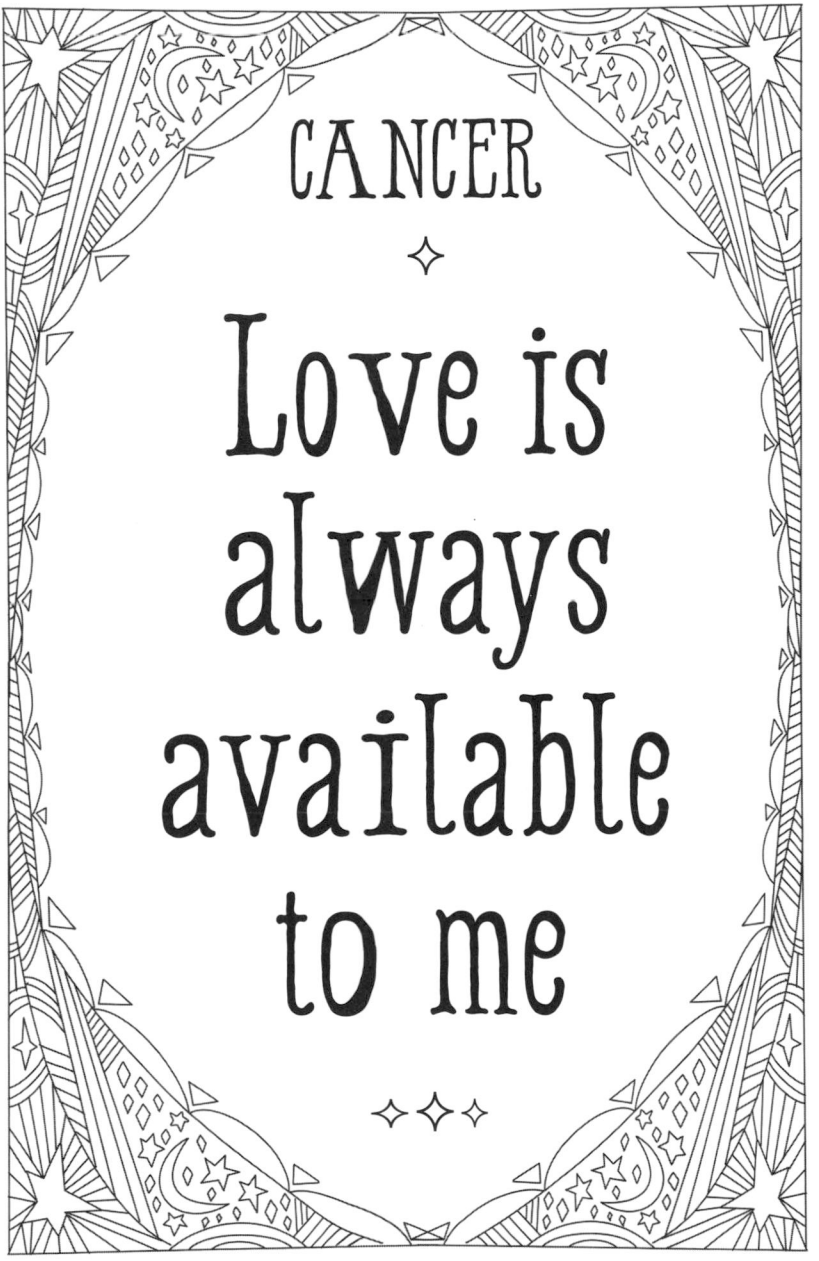
CANCER
Love is always available to me

Image by Andrea Lauren © Simon & Schuster, Inc.

Images by Andrea Lauren © Simon & Schuster, Inc., and 123RF/Volodymyr Horbovyy

Image by Andrea Lauren © Simon & Schuster, Inc.

summer

Image by Andrea Lauren © Simon & Schuster, Inc.

Cancer

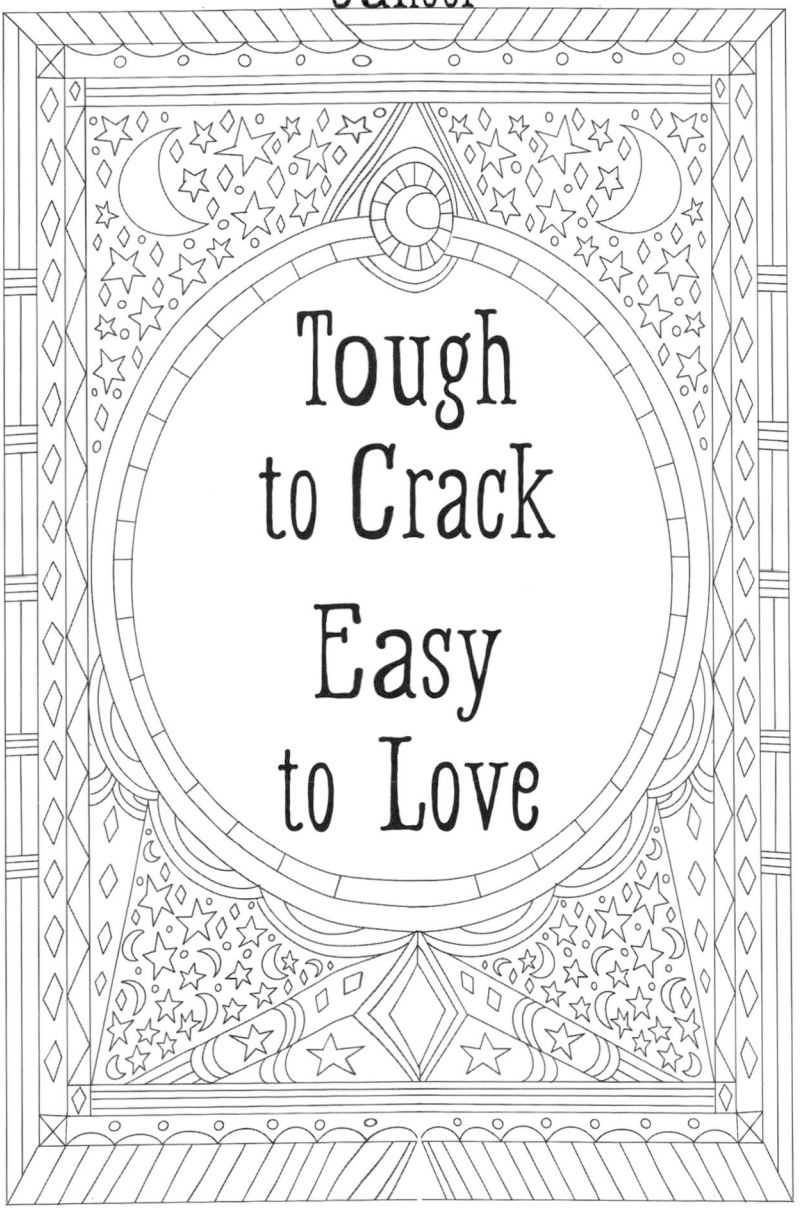

Image by Andrea Lauren © Simon & Schuster, Inc.

Cancer
Ruled by the Moon

Image by Andrea Lauren © Simon & Schuster, Inc.

Cancer

Images by Andrea Lauren © Simon & Schuster, Inc., and 123RF/Volodymyr Horbovyy

Kind
INTUITIVE
Protective
DEVOTED
PASSIONATE

Image by Andrea Lauren © Simon & Schuster, Inc.

Images by Andrea Lauren © Simon & Schuster, Inc., and 123RF/Volodymyr Horbovyy

Image by Andrea Lauren © Simon & Schuster, Inc.

RULING
HOUSE
4
The House of
Family & Home

Image by Andrea Lauren © Simon & Schuster, Inc.

Cancer
I Trust
MY
Intuition

Images by Andrea Lauren © Simon & Schuster, Inc., and 123RF/Volodymyr Horbovyy

Images © 123RF/Volodymyr Horbovyy and Getty Images/KavalenkavaVolha

Images by Andrea Lauren © Simon & Schuster, Inc., and 123RF/Volodymyr Horbovyy

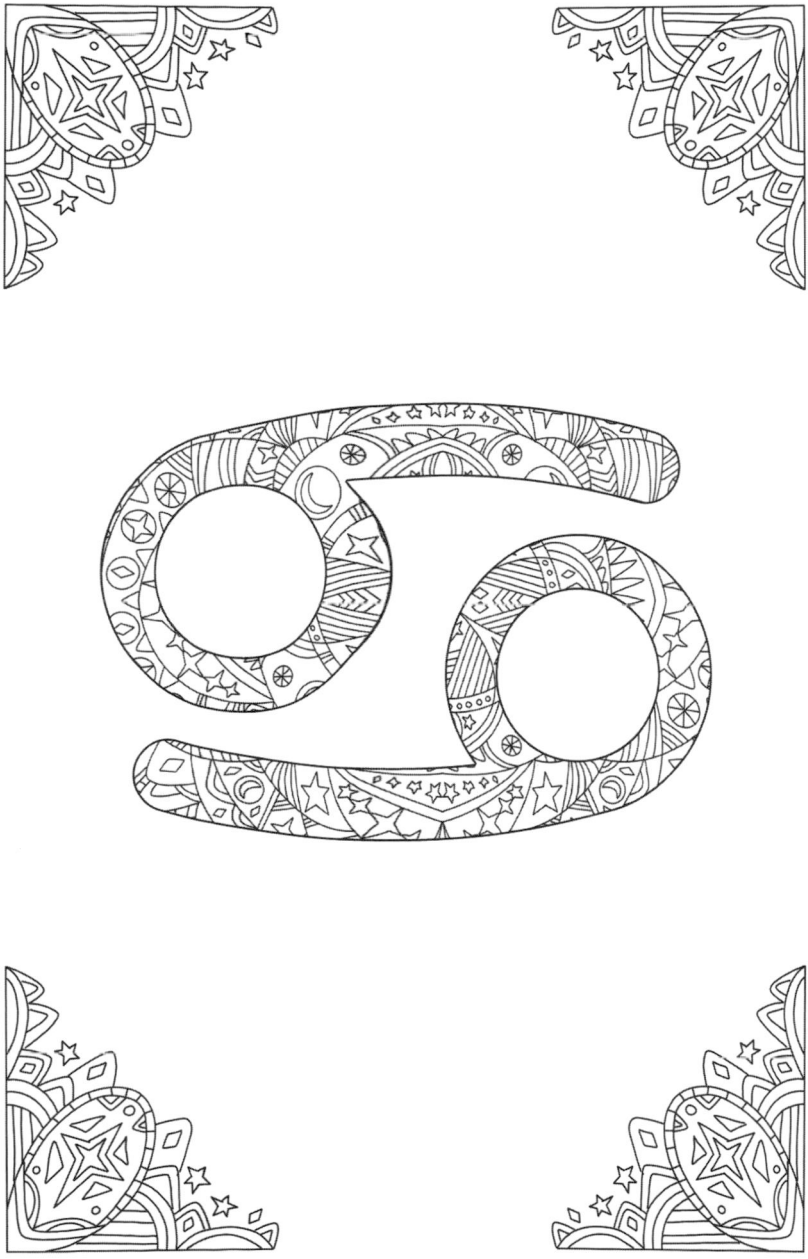

Image by Andrea Lauren © Simon & Schuster, Inc.

CANCER

Images © Getty Images/ElenaLux and 123RF/kotoffei

Aries
Taurus
Gemini
Cancer
Leo
Virgo
Libra
Scorpio
Sagittarius
Capricorn
Aquarius
Pisces

Images by Andrea Lauren © Simon & Schuster, Inc., and 123RF/Volodymyr Horbovyy

Water Signs

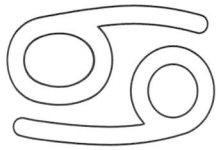

Cancer

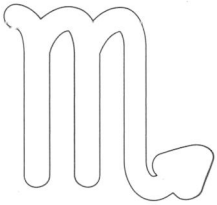

Scorpio

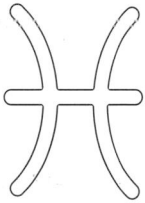

Pisces

Images by Andrea Lauren © Simon & Schuster, Inc., and 123RF/Volodymyr Horbovyy

LET THE STARS LEAD THE WAY

Image by Andrea Lauren © Simon & Schuster, Inc.